“Jesus the Abuser and the Man Who Listens to Dogs

A novel by Ivan Valle.”

Dedication

For those who trembled without a name.
For those who made others tremble,
like Jesus the Abuser:
may no silence protect them forever.

Jesus the Abuser and the Man Who Listens to Dogs

First edition, 2026

ISBN: 979-8-9940732-5-4

Printed in the United States of America

PROLOGUE

They wear crosses around their necks.
They greet people.
They help their neighbors.
They say "good morning."

They seem proper.

They use faith as an alibi.
Habit as a mask.
Morality as a shield.

With one hand they bless.
With the other, they harm.

This book is not about justice.
Justice requires witnesses.

Nor is it about redemption.
Redemption demands repentance.

It is about two ways of being in the world:

the way of those who turn another's trembling into a trade, and the way of those who, even when tired, still stop to listen.

One leaves marks on bodies.
The other learns how to read them.

Between them, the animals.

And something even more fragile:

the idea that pain,
if it is covered with a cross
and spoken in decent words,
ceases to exist.

CHAPTER 1 — The Procession

In Holy Week, Miami does not become a temple.

It becomes a stage.

Not because faith is false,
but because pain, when repeated too often, begins to look like custom.

Crosses dragged like old furniture.
Chains like accessories.
Knees on asphalt.
T-shirts torn in the exact place where the wound can be seen.

The city breathes differently.

It smells of sweat, cheap incense, beer kept in coolers, dead flowers.

Families sit on folding chairs as if waiting for a parade.
Water vendors walk slowly.
Phones rise into the air.
Children get bored.

And through all of it walks a man carrying a cross.

No robe.
No crown.

Barefoot,
skin burned dark by the sun,
arms marked with ink that does not belong to prayer.

The cross is heavier than it should be.

Not because of the wood.

Because of how it is used.

He walks slowly.

Not from devotion.

From calculation.

Pain is more effective when it can be seen.

Every few steps he adjusts his grip.
The wood bites into his shoulder.

Someone whispers his name.

Someone else makes the sign of the cross.

A woman kneels as he passes.

He does not look at her.

He looks past her.

At the space her body leaves behind.

At the distance between people.

At exits.

A man murmurs:

“Poor soul.”

Another says:

“God bless him.”

Phones record.

Photos freeze the moment.

Suffering becomes content.

The man carrying the cross breathes through his mouth.

Slow.

Measured.

Under the shirt, the skin tells a different story:

numbers, crooked letters, small wars drawn in ink, names misspelled on purpose.

And across his back, covering everything:

the face of Jesús Malverde.

Saint of traffickers.
Protector of those who shoot first.

Christ in front.

Malverde behind.

Redemption on the chest.

Permission on the spine.

A boy watches from the sidewalk.

Big eyes.
Mouth open.

The man likes that look.

Respect without questions.

He walks past.

The crowd opens.

Then closes again.

Like water around a stone.

No one smells the metal.

No one hears the short breaths.

No one counts the silences.

They see the cross.

That is enough.

At the end of the street, someone shouts:

“Stay strong!”

A hand touches his arm.

The cross moves slightly.

Pain climbs his neck like electricity.

He smiles.

Not from gratitude.

From effect.

The procession continues.

Behind him, the city returns to its rhythm:

plates,
voices,
radios,
engines starting.

Normal life.

Clean on the surface.

And somewhere else in the city, two houses away from Magnolia Street,
a dog lifts its head in the dark.

It does not bark.

It does not know how.

It only breathes.

Badly.

ACT I — The Noise That Must Not Exist
Where pain learns to stay silent.

CHAPTER 2 — The Favor

Jesus the Abuser did not go into the yard.

He stayed in the kitchen, standing, his back against the unplugged refrigerator, listening.

From there, everything could be heard.

The metal.
The water.
The fast breathing.

Not the screams.

Those did not last.

On the table there was a glass with something transparent that was not water.

He did not touch it.

A man came in from the yard, drying his hands with a dirty rag.

"It's done," he said.

Jesus nodded.

He did not ask what.

He never asked.

He took a small bundle of bills from his pocket, folded many times.

He did not count them.

He left them on the table the way one leaves a tool.

The man took them without looking at him.

“Tomorrow they’ll bring another one.”

Jesus shrugged.

“Not here.”

“No.”

Silence.

From the yard came a dull thud.

Like wood against concrete.

Jesus blinked once.

Just once.

“And the boy?” the man asked.

Jesus took a moment to answer.

“He’s good for carrying.”

"He's a kid."

"Even better."

The other man did not argue.

He put the money away.

"On Thursday the ones from the south are coming."

Jesus took his jacket.

"Let me know beforehand."

He walked toward the door.

Before leaving, he looked at the sink.

Dark hairs were stuck to the drain.

He pushed them with his finger until they disappeared.

He opened the door.

On the street, the night was still normal.

A television on in a neighboring house.
A car passing slowly.
A woman watering plants as if nothing were happening behind those walls.

Jesus got into the car.

Turned the music on.

Loud.

As always.

So that noise would be the only thing visible.

And he drove off.

In the yard, someone was washing the ground with a hose.

The water ran into the drain.

Without a name.

CHAPTER 3 — The Things That Do Not Fit on a Form

In the morning, the man was in his garden.
It was not large.
Three meters of damp soil, aligned pots, two young trees protected with mesh.

He worked slowly.
Gloves on.
Knees on the ground.

He cut dry leaves with small, clean scissors, as if each plant were a minor wound that must not be allowed to worsen.

Flowers make no noise.
That was why he liked them.

When he finished, he washed his hands with a hose and sat for a moment to look at the new color of a bougainvillea.

Then he took the notebook.
Folded it.
Put on a clean shirt.
And walked to the police station.

The building was low, with air conditioning set too cold and walls covered in old notices.

He waited.

No one was in a hurry.

A young officer attended to him without standing up.

"How can I help you?"

The man took out the notebook.
He did not open it yet.

"Backyard. Two houses north on Magnolia Street," he said.
"Metal cage. Dog with training wounds."

The officer wrote something down.

"Did you see a fight?"

"No."

"Weapons?"

"No."

"People?"

"I heard one."

The officer put down his pen.

"Do you have photos?"

"Yes."

"Video?"

"Yes."

"Exact address?"

"He gave it."

The officer typed slowly.

"With that, we can open a report," he said, "but if the property owner denies the animal is his, it's difficult to intervene immediately."

The man nodded.

"There are also small animals used as bait."

The officer looked up for a second.

"Cats?"

"Yes."

The young man glanced around and lowered his voice.

"Look, sir… this falls more under animal control than criminal matters."

"There are bets."

"Did you see them?"

"No."

"Then it's a suspicion."

Silence.

The man rested his hands on the counter.
They were hands with dirt under the nails.
They did not tremble.

"The dog is not going to heal on its own."

The officer sighed.

"I can file the report."

He printed it.
Slid it across.

"If there's a repeat, call."

The man took the paper.
Folded it carefully.

"How many times?"

"Excuse me?"

"How many times does it have to happen?"

The young man shrugged.

"I don't know."

That was all.

On the way back, he stopped at a gardening store.

He bought black soil.
Seeds.
A mild fertilizer.

In his yard, he dug a small hole.

He planted something that would take years to give shade.

He watered it.

He sat again.

Watched the water sink into the dry soil.

He thought of the dog.
He thought of the cage.
He thought of the report folded inside his pocket.

He did not think about the war.
He never did.

He had learned that the world was not destroyed only by explosions.
Sometimes it was organized.
Like a poorly designed garden.

He said softly:

“They don’t care to see it alive.
Only that it doesn’t show when it dies.”

He returned to his plants.

The only things that still responded without asking for proof.

CHAPTER 4 — The Investigators' Office

The office smelled of reheated coffee and damp paper.
Not of blood.
Not of fear.
Of paperwork.

Four desks pushed together, separated by low filing cabinets like poorly planned trenches. On the walls: maps with old thumbtacks, notices about new protocols, outdated calendars.

A fan spun without deciding anything.

Detective Morales drank from a paper cup.

Cold coffee.

He knew it.

Still, he swallowed it.

"Another report without photos," he said, dropping a folder onto the desk.

No one looked up.

Agent Ruiz kept typing.

"Animals again?"

"Yes."

"Dead?"

"Not confirmed."

"Injured people?"

"No."

Silence.

Keys.

Paper.

The fan.

Ruiz checked a box on the form.

"Then it doesn't qualify as high priority."

Morales sat down.

"They talk about fights."

"They always do."

"About betting."

"There's always betting."

Morales rubbed his face.

"A guy came into the station today. Clean garden. Dirt under his nails. Former military, I think."

“Did he bring evidence?”

“No.”

Ruiz closed the file with a dry snap.

“Then he brought a story.”

Morales looked at the ceiling.

An old stain, shaped like a badly drawn country.

“He said they use cats.”

No one answered.

The silence thickened.

Uncomfortable.

From another desk someone murmured:

“That’s animal control.”

Ruiz nodded.

“And civil protection, at most.”

Morales lowered his voice.

“The neighborhood is afraid.”

She looked at him for the first time.

Not harshly.

With fatigue.

"The neighborhood is always afraid."

"This one is different."

"It always is for someone."

Morales opened another folder.

Theft photos.

Charts.

A narcotics report.

A major fraud case.

"We have three unsolved homicides," Ruiz said. "A shooting last night. A judge pushing for results. Elections in six months."

Morales closed the animal folder.

Slowly.

Like someone putting away something that is still breathing.

"So…"

Ruiz finished:

“Then not now.”

The fan kept turning.

Someone laughed in another office.

A printer jammed.

Morales wrote on the cover:

PENDING – LOW PRIORITY

The folder ended up under others.

Under numbers.

Under more useful dead bodies.

Ruiz stood up to get more coffee.

“You want some?”

Morales shook his head.

He looked at his empty cup.

“No.”

Violence did not disappear.

It only learned how to wait in the right folder.

CHAPTER 5 – The Neighborhood When He Passes

He did not announce his arrival.

There was no need.

The neighborhood learned it by reflex.

A woman turned the corner early, as if she had remembered something urgent.
A man closed his gate with two extra turns, even though it was not night.
In the store, the hand giving change trembled just enough to make a mistake.

"Keep it," the shopkeeper said. "It's fine."

It never was.

A child dropped his ball.

He did not run after it.

He let it die at the edge of the sidewalk.

The houses lowered their volume.

Not completely.

Just enough so that no one could say it was because of him.

Jesus the Abuser walked slowly.

Not out of fatigue.

Out of management.

He knew fear worked better when it was not rushed.

Clean T-shirt.
New sneakers.
A large fake watch, shining like a cheap promise.

He did not look into people's eyes.

He looked at the spaces around their faces.

As if counting exits.

As if measuring bodies without touching them.

A woman crossed the street holding her daughter's hand.

She squeezed harder.

Too hard.

The girl complained softly.

Jesus did not smile.

There was no need.

The effect was already done.

In a window, a curtain moved slightly.

Then it stayed still.

As if someone had stopped breathing behind it.

The entire neighborhood rehearsed an old choreography:

not seeing,
not knowing,
not being.

A dog barked in the distance.

A single bark.

Then silence.

Jesus stopped in front of an ordinary house.

It was not his.

It was not important.

He looked at the door the way one looks at a stone in the road.

Then he continued.

The neighborhood released its breath little by little.

Like a body surviving a minor accident.

In the store, the shopkeeper sat down.

Wiped the sweat with his forearm.

"He's gone," he told himself.

But it was not true.

Nothing went away.

It only settled.

From his garden, the ex-Ranger saw him cross at the end of the street.

He did not raise his hand.

He made no gesture.

Jesus did not look at him either.

He did not want to.

When he turned the corner, the neighborhood recovered its small noises:

dishes,
radios,
a brief laugh,
a weak argument.

Normality returned.

Like a clean bandage over a dirty wound.

And no one said anything.

Because the neighborhood had no dogs.

And that, for a long time now, explained everything.

CHAPTER 6 — The Black Car

The ex-Ranger was watering his plants when the car passed slowly.

Black.
Windows down.
Music inside.
Breathing outside.

Jesus the Abuser was driving with one hand on the wheel, the other hanging loose.

He did not honk.

He did not speed up.

He simply passed.

The Ranger did not lower his head.

He did not move.

He did not change the rhythm of the water falling onto the soil.

He lifted his eyes.

And looked at him.

Not the way one looks at danger.

The way one looks at a piece.

At something that has already been counted.

The car went on.

But in the side mirror, Jesus managed to see his own face.

The color drained from it in seconds.

From sun-burned skin, hard, street-tough…

to a pale, purplish, sickly tone.

He swallowed.

Clenched his teeth.

Accelerated.

That night, the ex-Ranger wrote a single line in his notebook:

He has no dog.

He closed the notebook.

Went to the sink.

Washed his hands calmly.

Like after touching something that was already dead.

From the neighboring yard came a brief metallic sound.

Then nothing.

The ex-Ranger returned to his plants.

The leaves were not trembling.

That was enough.

CHAPTER 7 — The Debt

That night he did not water the plants.

He stood in the kitchen, his hands resting on the sink, listening to the old refrigerator do its job without anyone asking it to.

He saw the black car again.

Not the face.
Not the music.

The shape.

The way it occupied the street as if the street were an extension of the body.

He thought, without emotion:

it was so little.
an unidentified piece of trash.
as every abuser is.

He did not notice when he tightened his grip on the glass.

The crystal split open in his hand without a sound.

His fingers passed over the broken edge as if through soft butter.

He watched the blood come out slowly, orderly, clean.

He said nothing.

He took a cloth.

Wrapped it.

As if it were soda spilled on the table.

Nothing more.

Then the memory returned.

Not complete.

It never came complete.

Dark water.
Weight on his chest.
A leg that did not respond.

And a pull.

Fabric tearing.

Teeth that did not attack.
That held.

Then air.

Then cold.

Then the world returning without asking permission.

The ex-Ranger opened the drawer.

The old leash was still there.

Cracked leather.
The smell of dust.

He did not touch it.

He closed the drawer slowly.

He did not think about justice.

He thought about the yard.

About the cage.

About the dog breathing badly.

He sat at the table.

Waited for dawn.

ACT II — The Cage Moves

CHAPTER 8 — Three Days Later: The Yard That Was Too Clean

The ex-Ranger walked down Magnolia Street again three days later.

Not at night.
In the morning.

The sun made visible what darkness hid more effectively: normality.

The houses were open.
A man was washing his car.
A woman was shaking out a rug.
A child was eating cereal, sitting on the steps of a front porch.

The yard of the house was still a mess.

A car without wheels resting on blocks.
Rusted doors.
Warped tables with old bottle rings.
Broken chairs.
Crushed cans sunk into the dirt.

Iron, dust, abandonment.

Nothing had changed there.

Except one thing.

In the middle of the chaos there was a clean rectangle.

Too clean.

Turned soil, darker than the rest of the ground, like a recent wound someone had tried to close with their hands.

There was no cage.
No chain.
No bucket.

The ex-Ranger stopped across the street.

He did not cross.

He looked.

He counted the steps from the fence to the back door.

Measured the distance between the lemon tree and the wall.

Noted the new invisible order of things.

There were no remains.

No blood.

No hair.

That meant two things:

either the dog was dead,
or it was no longer visible.

Both served the same purpose.

From a window, someone watched him.

A curtain moved slightly.

The ex-Ranger lifted his eyes.

The curtain closed.

He kept walking.

He did not look back.

Not out of bravery.

Out of economy.

At the corner, a garbage truck lifted a bag and dropped it with a dull thud.

A shapeless sound.

Like a small body falling badly.

The ex-Ranger went on without quickening his pace.

But the notebook in his pocket began to weigh on him.

Not because of the paper.

Because of what could not yet be written.

He stopped once more.

Looked at the clean rectangle inside the junkyard.

And said to himself, without emotion:

"Either it's dead… or it's no longer visible."

It was not sadness.

It was classification.

CHAPTER 9 — The Man Without a Dog

Jesus the Abuser had not slept well for three days.

Not from guilt.

From noise.

Not outside.

Inside.

A small, constant buzzing.

Like a fly trapped inside the skull that never gives up.

He woke before dawn.

Opened the refrigerator.
Closed it.

Opened a cabinet.
Closed it.

He ate without hunger.
Drank without taste.

And checked the yard.

The yard was his territory.

His signature.

His way of saying:

I rule here.

But now the yard had a problem.

A man had looked at him.

Not like a man looks at a man.

Like someone looks at an object.

At something with no history.

Only function.

That would not let him rest.

He would never say it out loud.

Not even to himself.

The yard was the same dump as always:

the car without wheels,
the beer-stained tables,
the rusted doors,
the crushed cans,
the hard soil where nothing grew.

He liked that disorder.

It felt honest.

What he did not like was order.

The cage was no longer outside.

That was the problem.

Now it was inside.

Two nights after disappearing from the yard,

the dog was breathing under a roof.

The dog was still alive.

That was what mattered.

He repeated it like a prayer without faith:

As long as the dog breathes, everything breathes.

On the third day, the dog stopped whining.

Not because it was better.

Because it learned.

Jesus heard its breathing.

Bad air.

Thick.

Like the air he had felt in the liquor store before the gunshot.

The memory disgusted him.

That night he went to the corner store.

He did not buy alcohol.

He bought curtains.

Thick.

Dark.

The owner looked at him strangely.

“Moving?”

Jesus smiled.

“Fixing things.”

At home, he hung the curtains without patience.

Bent nails.
Dry hammer blows.

He wanted it finished.

Like someone covering a hole before the water rises.

Then he went to the yard.

Looked at the familiar chaos.

Then at the cage.

The dog looked back.

Not with fear.

With tired calculation.

Jesus felt the need to prove something.

He yanked the yard door open.

The gate screeched.

He liked the sound.

It reminded him he could still cause effect.

He grabbed the chain.

Shook it.

Metal answered.

For one second, the world aligned again:

cause,
effect,
obedience.

Then he remembered:

the open notebook,
the quiet man,
the silence that cannot be bought.

The heat left his chest.

Jesus released the chain.

“Inside,” he said.

Not to the dog.

To the future.

That same night he dragged the cage into the house.

Not the living room.

A side room.

Cold tiles.

The dog hit the bars.

It did not bark.

He liked that.

The obedient silence.

He closed the door.

Placed a chair against the handle.

Not for safety.

For ritual.

Then he turned off the music.

That was the strangest part.

He sat in the living room with the television on mute.

Blue light filled his hands like dead water.

He listened.

Behind the door:

metal.

A nail.

A chain.

A body adjusting to space that was not enough.

Jesus sat.

Did not pray.

Did not think.

He waited.

As if time would give instructions.

And for the first time in years,

the house did not feel like his.

It felt like a larger cage.

CHAPTER 10 – First Face-to-Face (Magnolia)

At the next corner, he was there.

Leaning against a black car.

He was not smoking.
Not talking.
Not making any noise.

The music was not playing.

That was new.

The ex-Ranger recognized him without surprise.
The way one recognizes the final piece before touching it.

He stopped two meters away.

He did not extend his hand.
He did not greet him.
He did not say his name.

The wind moved an old piece of paper across the asphalt.

Nothing else.

Jesus.

He knew it by the body.

Not by the face.

There are men who look to fight.
Others to negotiate.

This one looked to measure.

That was worse.

"Are you looking for something?" Jesus said.

The voice came out firm.
Practiced for years in small rooms.

The other did not answer.

The ex-Ranger

Looked first at the car.

Then at the clean sneakers.
The large watch.
The scarred knuckles.

Then the eyes.

He did not find anger there.

He found hunger.

He took out the notebook.
Opened it.

He did not write anything.

He only held it open.

The way one holds a document that does not need to be read.

Jesus

Felt the movement under his ribs.

Not fear.

Anger without direction.

"There's nothing here."

The silence continued.

"What are you looking at?"

Nothing.

"You don't know me."

Nothing.

Jesus took a step forward.

The other did not step back.

"Are you threatening me?"

The air did not change.

"Then leave."

The ex-Ranger

Closed the notebook.
Put it in his back pocket.

He stayed still one second longer.

Just one.

As if finishing counting something invisible.

Then he turned.

And walked away.

Jesus

Followed him with his eyes.

Not to the end of the street.

Only as far as it was still useful to observe.

That night he did not play music.

He drank in silence.

He looked at his hands.

He remembered the clean rectangle inside the junkyard.

He remembered the thin dog that no longer cried out.

He could not sleep.

And at three twelve he woke up.

Without knowing why.

He listened.

Nothing.

But his chest sounded as if someone were breathing badly inside.

CHAPTER 11 – Normal Life

The next morning, Jesus did what he always did.

He got up.
Washed his face without looking too closely.

The water was warm and, for a second, the steam smelled like rust.

He stayed with his hands resting on the sink, waiting for his body to give him an instruction.

None came.

He dried himself.
Got dressed.

Simple T-shirt.
Simple pants.
Shoes without shine.

Normality was his best disguise.

Not because he sought it.

Because it already lived in him like an old habit: breathing, walking, paying, smiling when required.

In the kitchen he drank coffee without sugar.

He liked the bitterness.

He liked feeling something scrape his tongue.

He opened the door.

The air was cold and clean.

A January sky, clear as a well-told lie.

He walked down the sidewalk at an even pace.

Neither fast.
Nor slow.

The exact rhythm of someone who does not want to be remembered.

At the corner, the usual woman was watering her plants.

Jesus said:

"Good morning."

She looked at him, recognized him, answered in the same tired voice:

"Good morning, son."

"Son."

The word crossed his stomach like a badly swallowed object.

He kept walking.

At the grocery store, the man behind the counter raised his hand.

"Heeey, Jesus!"

The sound crossed his chest like a mild electric shock.

It was not the same "heeey" from the dream.

But it was close enough.

Jesus smiled.

Not out of joy.

Out of reflex.

"Everything okay?" the man asked.

"Everything's fine."

The perfect sentence.

It opens nothing.
Closes nothing.
Promises nothing.

He paid for the bread.

Put away the coins.

Went out.

On the next block he saw a stray dog.

Young.
Dirty fur.
One lame leg.

It sniffed a trash bag patiently, as if reading.

Jesus stopped.

Not for long.

Just enough to make it look normal to stop.

The dog lifted its head.

Its eyes had no fear.

No hatred.

They had distance.

The exact measure between two bodies that owe each other nothing.

Jesus felt the faint impulse to approach.

Not out of affection.

Out of control.

He did not do it.

He had learned long ago not to move when desire is too clear.

He kept walking.

The dog watched him until he disappeared.

At work, Jesus was proper.

He greeted people.

Listened.

Nodded.

Did what he had to do without asking why.

He was efficient.

And efficiency is often confused with virtue.

People like men who do not disturb.

Because that way they do not have to look at themselves.

A coworker asked him about his mother.

“She’s fine,” he said.

He did not know if it was true.

It was not a lie.

It was habit.

His boss gave him an extra task.

Jesus accepted it.

"You're reliable," the man said.

"Reliable."

That made him laugh inside.

Outside he only said:

"Thank you."

Trust is a gift given so no one has to watch.

In the middle of the afternoon he went outside to get some air.

Behind the building there was dirt, a dumpster, and a small puddle where dead leaves floated.

And there, again, the dog.

Maybe the same one.

Lame.

Still.

Jesus looked at it.

The dog did not come closer.

Did not beg.

Did not humiliate itself.

It only held the distance.

Jesus searched his pocket.

He had a piece of bread.

He left it on the ground.

Not too close.
Not too far.

He waited.

As if giving an order without a voice.

The dog moved forward.

Took the bread.

Moved back.

Jesus felt a brief satisfaction.

Not kindness.

Response.

He stood up.

Went back inside.

That night, when he returned to the neighborhood, children were playing with a deflated ball.

One fell.

Scraped his knee.

Cried.

The mother came out shouting:

“Look at you! You’re always the same!”

She wiped the blood roughly.

“Heeey… stop that nonsense.”

The sound came back.

Heeey.

Jesus stopped.

He did not intervene.

He did not approach.

He watched.

He saw that the crying was not only pain.

It was shame.

He saw that the woman was not only a mother.

She was repetition.

He saw that the child was learning something faster than how to walk:

to apologize for bleeding.

Jesus understood something with cold clarity:

people do not change.

They are inherited.

The child stopped crying.

Not because he calmed down.

Because he arranged himself.

Jesus kept walking.

At home he ate dinner alone.

Turned on the television without sound.

The blue light filled the room like an aquarium.

He sat down.

He did not think.

Thinking was touching the bottom.

And he preferred to float.

But that night sleep had left a crack.

Through the crack came things:

the dog,
the chain,
ten feet,
ten years,
the white hen trembling in his hands,
his father's voice saying *time* as if it were a natural sentence.

Jesus went to the bathroom.

Washed his hands.

Washed them too much.

As if water could erase a shape.

He looked at himself in the mirror for only one second.

To make sure he still had a human face.

He turned off the light.

Lay down.

The neighborhood was silent.

But it was not peace.

It was surveillance.

Before falling asleep, something formed in his chest.

Not guilt.

A question.

Animal.

Simple.

Without forgiveness:

What if one day the world stops obeying?

The dog, somewhere in the night, kept walking without making a sound.

CHAPTER 12 – The First Bullet

Days after the cage was moved.

Jesus the Abuser was not looking for courage.
He was looking for anesthesia.

He pushed the liquor store door open with his shoulder.
The bell rang once. Tired.

Inside, the air smelled of old sugar, warm glass, and recycled nights.

He walked to the bottles without checking prices.
His fingers brushed the neck of a rum bottle. Cold. Perfect.
He took it down. Put it back.

As if he couldn't decide which hand to use.

Behind the counter stood a thin man.
Bare arms.
Still eyes.

Not tired.
Still.

Jesus stepped forward and waited for what always came:

the space shrinking,
the gaze lowering,
the world arranging itself around his shape.

It didn't happen.

The clerk looked at him the way you look at a chair.

A thing.

Something that doesn't demand anything.

Jesus swallowed.
His hand went to his waist by reflex, as if his identity lived there.

He took nothing out.

He only remembered who he was supposed to be.

He spat an inherited insult.
Bent. Old.
Thrown like a fake coin to buy respect.

The clerk didn't argue.
Didn't smile.

He placed the rag on the counter and rested both hands flat.
Separated.
Marking distance.

Jesus took half a step forward.
The sticky floor grabbed his sole.

The bell trembled again as someone entered and left quickly, as if the air itself were afraid to stay.

"What are you looking at?" Jesus said.

Nothing.

That “nothing” wasn’t a word.

It was a gap.

One second.
Maybe two.

Jesus felt his chest open from the inside.

Not anger.

Vertigo.

The gunshot came after.

Dry.
Short.
Real.

As if someone had turned off the music of the world with one finger.

The impact threw him back.
He crashed into a shelf.

Bottles rang like a broken bell.

Glass against glass.

A drop fell on his wrist.

He didn’t know if it was liquor or blood.

First, burning.

Then dark heat opening inside him.

He grabbed the counter.
Slipped.
Dropped to his knees.

And then something happened that he would never tell:

he wet himself.

Right there.

Between beer boxes and cheap bottles.

No chase.
No fight.
No story.

The clerk didn't approach.

Didn't celebrate.

He only stepped back,
like someone putting a dangerous tool aside
and waiting for it to shut down by itself.

Jesus staggered out, clutching his side.

The door hit his shoulder on the way out.
The bell rang again.

Almost mocking.

He walked two blocks without feeling them.

Entered his house.
Locked twice.

The lock went: *click.*

That sound gave him dirty peace.

He tore off his shirt.

In the bathroom, he turned the water on hard.
The mirror fogged.

He washed.
Washed again.

Pressed the wound with an old towel.

He trembled naked on the floor like a road-killed animal that still doesn't understand why it's alive.

He didn't pray.

Didn't call anyone.

Didn't scream.

He closed his eyes.

He saw the open notebook. Empty. Held like a mirror.
He saw the clerk's eyes.
He saw the clean rectangle in the yard.

He vomited.

Held the edge of the bathtub until his fingers went white.

In the corner of the room, where the light didn't quite reach,
something seemed to adjust itself.

Not a figure.
Not a body.

An absence darker than the wall.

The Shadow didn't touch anything.

It only watched the instrument learn, for the first time,
the exact shape of fear.

Days later, Jesus told another version on the corner.

That he shot first.
That the other man trembled.
That he had him under control.

They laughed.
They called him brave.

No one saw the wound leaking.

No one saw the night shaking.

No one saw how silence had become unbearable.

The street kept his lie.

He kept his truth:

his body was hard,
but his center was soft,

and all his violence was not enough to manufacture courage.

Only noise.

That night he began to think about covering his skin.

Like someone painting over a crack with black paint.

CHAPTER 13 – Animal Control Protocol

The phone rang three times before someone picked up.

"Services."

The voice was neutral.
Learned.

Morales spoke with his mouth full of coffee.

"I have a report from Magnolia. Possible fights. Injured animals. Should I forward it to animal control?"

On the other end there was a tired breath.
Keys.

"Is there visual material?"

"Yes."

A minimal pause.

"Photos?"

"Yes."

"Video?"

"Also."

More keys.

"Is the animal clearly visible?"

"Yes."

"Is the owner's face visible?"

"No."

"Exact address?"

"Yes."

"Name of the property owner?"

Morales looked at the paper.

"Jesus M. R."

The report was dated four days after the clean rectangle.

Keys again.

"Does Mr. Jesus M. R. acknowledge ownership of the animal?"

Morales squeezed the paper cup.

"No. He says it's not his."

"Is the animal still visible?"

"No."

Brief silence.

"Does the dog have visible identification?"

"No."

"Microchip?"

"No."

"Collar with information?"

"No."

The voice dropped half a tone.

"Then there is no proof of ownership."

Morales frowned.

"In previous reports the animal appears inside his property, in the closed rear area."

"Visible from the street?"

"No."

"Then it is inside the home or in a closed private area."

Morales closed his eyes for one second.

"It's injured."

"It is unidentified."

"There are videos."

“Of direct aggression by the owner?”

“No.”

“Of betting?”

“No.”

“Of money exchange?”

“No.”

The phrase came clean, administrative:

“Then there is a report of an injured animal, with no confirmed owner, and no legal access to the location.”

“And what does that mean?”

“That it falls under animal control.”

“And abuse?”

“Only if ownership is proven or a court order is obtained.”

“And if tomorrow it disappears?”

A short pause.

“Then there is no animal.”

Morales breathed through his nose.

“Name of the complainant?”

"A civilian."

"Background?"

"Former military, it seems."

Keys again.

"It is classified as 'possible loose animal on private property.'"

Morales looked at the wall.

"Nothing else?"

"Nothing else."

The line went dead.

Morales held the receiver one second longer, as if the plastic could offer another answer.

It did not.

He took two steps.
Sat back down.

Ruiz passed behind him with a new folder under her arm.

"What was it?"

"The same."

Ruiz nodded without stopping.

"Change the label."

"To what?"

"Night noise."

"Or problematic neighbor."

"Or loose animal."

Morales looked at the Magnolia report.

The printed photos.
The video frames.

The name: Jesus M. R.

In the system he was Jesus M. R.
In the neighborhood he was Jesus the Abuser.
On the street, Jesus Malverde.
In his belief, Jesus of Nazareth.

He remembered the hands with dirt.

The way they did not tremble.

The question:

"How many times does it have to happen?"

He wrote at the top, in blue ink:

NOISE / POSSIBLE LOOSE ANIMAL

He filed the document.

Not because he believed it.

Because the system breathed better when the words were small.

In another office someone laughed.

A printer spat out badly cut pages.

A television broadcast a news program with no sound.

On the screen, a politician moved his lips like an expensive fish.

Morales stood up to get more coffee.

The paper cup trembled slightly in his hand.

Not from emotion.

From weariness accumulated in the bones.

The Magnolia folder went into the second drawer.

Under a bank fraud.
Under a shooting.
Under two recent dead bodies.
Under numbers that did know how to defend themselves.

Violence had not disappeared.

It had only changed its name.

And now it slept peacefully,

inside a proper file.

CHAPTER 14 – The Cross, the Promise, and the Saint

Jesus the Abuser did not start carrying the cross after the wound.
He had been doing it before. Always.

He pulled it out of the room the way you pull out a heavy piece of furniture.
He dragged it a little and the wood scraped the floor.
He liked that sound: it proved presence.

Outside, during Holy Week, Miami was not a temple. It was a stage.
The street smelled of sweat, cheap incense, and beer kept in coolers.
Phones rose like modern candles.

Jesus settled the cross on his right shoulder.
The wood dug in where he was already used to it.
He clenched his jaw. Took the first step.

Not out of faith.
Out of structure.

The cross did two things: it took up space and it ordered the story.
People saw the wood first. Then the body. Never the other way around.

He walked slowly, letting pain be visible, useful.
Every ten steps he adjusted his grip. Splinters marked his

fingers.
A woman offered him water. He did not look at her. He only nodded with his chin.

Under the T-shirt, the skin said something else:
crooked numbers, small-war symbols, names misspelled on purpose.

And on his back, taking up everything, the face of Jesús Malverde.
The saint of traffickers.
The protector of those who shoot first.

Jesus felt the tattoo like a warm coat.

Christ in front.
Malverde behind.

Redemption on the chest.
Permission on the back.

A boy watched him from the sidewalk.
Jesus saw the wide eyes and the half-open mouth.
He liked that respect without questions.

He kept walking.

Christ was the public alibi.
Malverde the private authorization.

One cleaned the story.
The other enabled the facts.

There was also the other crucified man.

The one who died beside Christ.
The one who was forgiven without changing anything.

Jesus did not know his name.
He never learned it.

He only knew the idea:

that sometimes it is enough to hang correctly
to come out clean.

He liked that part of the story.

Not as faith.
As a system.

As a small door at the end of the hallway,
reserved for dirty men
who do not want to go back.

Someone shouted:

"God bless you!"

A hand touched his shoulder carefully.
The cross shifted one centimeter and pain shot up his neck
like electricity.

Jesus smiled.

Not out of gratitude.

Out of effect.

He thought in terms of balance.

The world—according to his crooked accounting—had given him:

hunger,
a father,
a chain,
humiliation.

That was a debt.

And every debt demands collection.

The cross served him to say without speaking:

I carry something too.

And that silent sentence washed him on the outside.

When the walk ended, he leaned the cross against a wall. The wood went *thunk*.

He rubbed his shoulder, as if removing a uniform.

Several women came closer.

“God bless you, mijo.”

Jesus lowered his head, accepting the blessing like a stamp.

A permit.

No one asked about the yard.
No one smelled the metal.
No one heard the torn air.

Jesus lifted the cross again, only to move it two steps.
The wood groaned against the floor once more.

And for one day, it was enough to feel clean on the outside.

Invisible on the inside.

CHAPTER 15 — The Woman Sees the Idiot

Jesus stood in front of the closet mirror.
Shirtless.

He flexed one arm. Then the other.
He turned his torso so the tattoos looked like they moved on their own.
The mirror returned a cheap catalog of threats.

The cross rested against the wall, tilted, like an old piece of furniture.
A splinter had come loose from the edge and he did not remove it, out of stubbornness.

She watched him from the doorway.
Not with fear. With fatigue.

"Are you done falling in love with yourself, or do you need one more pose?" she said.

Jesus smiled without turning around.
He ran his fingers over the tattoo on his chest as if smoothing an invisible shirt.

"Women like a strong man."

She walked in and sat on the edge of the bed.
She removed a bracelet and set it on the nightstand. The metal made a soft sound.
That small sound was more serious than any scream.

"Dogs like biting furniture too," she answered. "It doesn't mean they're intelligent."

Jesus frowned.
He opened a drawer and slammed it shut without taking anything out, as if he needed noise to exist.

"What's wrong with you today?"

She stared at him.
Her eyes did not tremble.

"That I'm tired."

"Tired of what?"

She took a deep breath. Stood up. Opened the closet.
She started taking out clothes without hurry, folding each thing methodically.
Like someone deciding to leave a room alive.

"Of living with a man who thinks he's a hurricane… and turns out to be a fan."

Jesus let out a short laugh.
He leaned on the mirror frame. The wood creaked.

"You talk pretty for someone poor."

She put a T-shirt into a bag.

"There's someone else."

Jesus blinked.
As if the word did not exist in his language.

"Someone else what?"

"A man."

Jesus stepped closer.
The bed sank into the mattress. The room got smaller.

"A joke?"

"No."

"A cousin?"

"No."

Jesus swallowed.
He looked at his tattoos, as if they were an argument.

"What's he like?"

She did not smile.

"Normal."

That was worse.

"Normal how?"

She said it calmly, blow by blow:

"No tattoos.
No speeches.
No need to look dangerous just to feel alive."

Jesus looked at his chest.
The numbers, the virgins, the guns, the crooked names.
Decoration.

"And what does he have that I don't?"

She thought for a second.
She zipped the bag. The *zzzip* sounded like a final seal.

"Straight posture."

Jesus laughed, but it didn't fully come out.

"I've got a back."

"No," she said. "You've got decoration."

He raised his voice.

"I'm the father of your kids!"

She didn't shout.
She swung the bag onto her shoulder and the strap tapped her collarbone: *tap*.

"And they've already learned to hide their toys when you get home."

Jesus went still.
That hurt more than the affair.

"Are you laughing at me?"

She shook her head, without hate.

"No. I'm mocking you because before I only had fear."

She opened the door.

"I can change," he said, almost out of air.

"You don't even know what you are."

Jesus looked at the cross. Then his arms. Then the floor.

"I'm a man."

She looked at him one last time.

"No.
You're a costume that thinks it's a body."

She left.

Jesus stayed alone.
Surrounded by muscles, by the cross, by the tattooed saint, by his portable legend.

He sat on the bed. Tried to flex again.
His arm trembled.

"Fuck..."

Under the bed, the butt of his fake gun stuck out.
Black plastic. Lying weight.
He pushed it back with his foot to hide it again.

From the adjoining room came a tiny sound: metal against tile.
The cage.

Jesus listened.
He did not go to see the dog.
He liked that low sound: it made him believe he could still order something.

He stayed sitting there, staring at the mirror.

And for the first time the mirror did not return a monster.

It returned a large piece of furniture.
Heavy.
With crooked legs.

And badly placed nails no one wanted to fix.

CHAPTER 16 – The Two Dreams

That same night, sleep took him like a fall.

Jesus the Abuser didn't fall asleep.

He dropped.

As into a well without walls.

No edge.
No descent.

Only damp darkness
and an old smell,
like rust mixed with ancient hunger.

He dreamed he was seventeen.

Not a child.
Not a man.

Seventeen:
old enough to carry weight,
too young to choose what to do with it.

The dog was there.

The family dog.

Not thin yet.
Not wounded.

Rough fur.
Clear eyes.
Ribs barely marked by the same emptiness chewing inside him.

A hen had escaped the coop.

White.
Clumsy.
Alive.

Jesus hunted it with stones.

Not for fun.
Not from rage.

From that dry pressure in the bones that water doesn't calm.

He grabbed it with clumsy hands.

Felt the small heart beating against his palm.

He twisted its neck.

Not fast.

Not clean.

The dog arrived afterward.

It smelled the blood.
The feathers.
The shaking.

Its tail moved.

Not to steal.

To ask.
To eat.
To continue being.

Then his father appeared.

He had already been there.

Always had.

He had come years earlier from the south.

Not to find work.

To erase himself.

He had crossed borders to leave behind games, fights, knives used at night,
names that were better forgotten.

He brought crime folded inside his body.

And turned it into habit.

Smelling of cheap alcohol.

With eyes broken on the inside.

He smiled.

No warmth.

“Look what you did, bastard.”

He didn’t say *animal*.

He said *bastard*.

He hit him.

Not hard.

Educational.

Like straightening a crooked table.

Then he brought the chain.

Ten feet.

He measured it with open arms.

“So you learn.”

He didn’t point at Jesus.

He pointed at the dog.

The dog was tied to the yard post.

It didn’t bite.

Didn’t run.

Didn't understand.

It sat.

It waited.

Years passed like fine dust.

The mother was gone.

She had left that same house, up north.

With another man.

Further north.

No letters.

No return.

Jesus stayed with the dog.

And the chain.

Ten years.

Ten feet of world.

The same circle of dirt.

The same radius.

The same sun splitting his back.

Jesus grew.

His voice hardened.
His back closed.
His eyes learned not to ask.

Twenty-seven.

One morning the dog didn't stand up.

It wasn't violent.

It wasn't dramatic.

Just a body that didn't complete the circle.

Jesus watched from the doorway.

He didn't come closer.

Didn't touch anything.

Something warm opened in his chest.

Not guilt.

Not grief.

Order.

The calm of understanding that pain can be stored in small spaces.

Measured.

Managed.

Turned into method.

The dog looked at him one last time.

Not afraid.

Not reproachful.

Faithful.

With that clean stupidity of animals
who still expect something good.

Jesus smiled.

Slowly.

Like someone finishing the learning of a trade.

He woke with a steady heart.

Dry.

Complete.

He didn't cry.

Jesus the Abuser never cried.

Elsewhere, at the same hour…

The ex-Ranger dreamed he was back in the crater.

The impact had been clean.

Mathematical.

The explosion was not fire.

It was silence.

A silence that pushes.

He was half buried in black water.

Cold.

So cold it burned.

Blood left his side, warm and thick,
mixing with the water like living ink.

He couldn't move his legs.

The rifle was still in his right hand.

He didn't remember picking it up.

But it was there.

As if the body knew things the mind abandons.

The dog appeared at the edge of the crater.

Covered in mud.

One ear torn.

Eyes alive.

Too alive for that dead landscape.

The Ranger tried to speak.

Only air came out.

The dog climbed down.

Slipped.

Hit stone.

Dragged itself.

Belly to rock.

Meter by meter.

The Ranger cried without tears.

Only with his face.

The dog reached him.

Smelled him.

Licked his hand once.

Then stopped.

Looked around.

Looked at the sky without sky.

Turned.

Ran.

Climbed out.

Escaped.

Lived.

The Ranger watched him go and smiled.

Smiled with blood-stained teeth.

And in the deepest place still intact inside him, he thought:

God bless him.
God protect him.
Thank you, dog.
Thank you, God.

He pulled the trigger.

Shot forward.

Not at an enemy.

Not at a shape.

Forward.

As if aiming at continuation.

The water grew colder.

The body farther away.

Then he heard the blades.

Sound before light.

A hammer turning in the sky.

The Ranger woke screaming:

“Where is the dog?”
“Where is the dog?”

The doctors didn’t understand.

No one answered.

Only the real helicopter, already there,
spinning over his head like a mechanical wound.

Jesus sat up in his bed.

The Ranger trembled on a stretcher, in another time, in another country.

Two men.

Two bodies.

Two geographies.

The same animal.

The same silence.

One learned pain could be managed.

The other learned pain could be accompanied.

One was the center of the chain.

The other, the edge of the crater.

And somewhere off the map,

the dog kept walking.

Free or not.

Alive.

That was the only thing that mattered.

When the ex-Ranger opened his eyes for real, he was not at war.

He was at home.

In his bed.

Feet on cold floor.

The clock said:

3:12.

He listened.

This time there was no whimper.

There was an idea.

One.

Operational.

Clean.

Irreversible:

to make one single test.

ACT III — The Substitution

CHAPTER 17 — The Proof That Does Fit on a Form

The ex-Ranger did not look for justice.

He looked for a format.

He had learned the essential thing: the system does not respond to truth.
It responds to what can be filed without shame.

That dawn, at 3:12, he did not get up on impulse.

He got up by calendar.

He dressed without turning on the light.
Took the keys.
Not the phone.

In the kitchen he opened a drawer.
Took out an empty manila envelope.
Wrote on it, in neat letters:

MAGNOLIA / NOISE

It was not the correct name.

It was the name the system accepted.

Outside, Florida was not dark.

It was humid.

He walked to the Magnolia corner without looking at houses,

like someone who does not want to wake the neighborhood,

like someone who does not want to owe explanations.

He did not cross immediately.

First he observed the street the way one observes a garden before pruning:

what changed,
what disappeared,
what had been "fixed" in a hurry.

The yard of Jesus the Abuser was still a disaster:

old cars, car parts, beer-stained tables, cans, torn bags, crooked chairs.

A permanent party without music.

But something did not fit.

A rectangle.

Turned soil, darker than the rest.

Too clean for that chaos.

As if someone had erased something with their hands.

The ex-Ranger did not approach.

He stayed on the opposite sidewalk.

Took out the notebook.

Wrote:

DAY 1 / 03:12 / NO DOG VISIBLE / TURNED SOIL / GARBAGE TRUCK 04:40

Same week. Same neighborhood. Another shift of the same silence.

He put the notebook away.

Walked one block more and sat on a bench.

Waited.

At 4:38 the truck arrived.

At 4:40 it stopped in front of Jesus the Abuser's house.

Three bags.

One heavier than the others.

He did not see blood.

He did not see hair.

He did not see anything.

But he heard the thud.

The sound of a bag falling without air.

The Ranger did not write "body."

He wrote:

04:40 / HARD BAG / 3 BAGS / SAME-DAY PICKUP

That afternoon, unhurried, he went to the corner store.

He bought two things:

— A new notebook.
— A can of white paint.

The clerk looked at him oddly.

"Painting your house?"

The ex-Ranger said:

"I mark plants."

A useful lie.

On his way out, he noticed the shopping cart of the owner of the yard next to Jesus the Abuser's.

An older man, trembling hands, eyes lowered.

The ex-Ranger nodded to him.

Did not ask anything.

Questions kill witnesses.

He walked home.

Watered his garden.

Planted a seed.

That night, at his table, he prepared the evidence.

Not like a hero.

Like a file clerk.

He attached to the manila envelope:

— Dates.
— Times.
— License plate of the truck (seen from the bench).
— Collection route.
— Three neighbor "noise" notes (no names, only initials).
— One single photograph: the clean rectangle inside the chaotic yard.

One photo.

Not of a dog.

Of a pattern.

At the end he wrote a short, administrative sentence:

"Possible animal abuse / repeated circumstantial evidence / request welfare check."

The Ranger sealed the envelope.

And for the first time in months, he did not feel rage.

He felt precision.

CHAPTER 18 – Clean Operation

The inspection arrived mid-morning.

Not out of urgency.

Because there was room in the schedule.

Two vans.
One uniformed officer.
A woman from Animal Control with new gloves.
A supervisor who looked at his watch as if the watch were the only victim.

Morales went with them, the folder in his hand.
Ruiz did not come.

"What do we have?" the supervisor asked.

Morales opened the folder.

"Repeated reports. Fixed schedule. A 'heavy' bag in the trash. Possible injured dog."

"Photos of the animal?" the supervisor asked.

Morales swallowed.

"No."

The Animal Control woman sighed.

"Then we go for a 'welfare check.' We knock. If no one opens, we close."

The van stopped in front of the house.

The yard was a disaster.
Half-dismantled cars.
Party tables.
Cans.
Garbage.

And yet, everything was… prepared.

As if the filth had been arranged.

A man came out through the side door.

Easy smile.
Clean work shirt.
Hands that did not tremble.

"Good morning, officers. Is something wrong?"

Morales watched him for a second.

It was not Jesus the Abuser.

It was another man.

The "proper" one.

The one who knows how to speak to police.

The supervisor showed a paper.

“We’re here for an animal welfare inspection.”

The man opened his hands theatrically.

“There are no animals here. No dogs. No cats. Nothing.”

The Animal Control woman looked at the yard.

“May we come in?”

“Of course.”

They entered.

The chaos was where it was supposed to be: outside.

Inside, the house was surprisingly clean.

Thick curtains.
Strong air conditioning.
The smell of fresh bleach.

The Animal Control woman walked down the hallway.

Stopped.

Listened.

Nothing.

She opened a door.

An empty room.
No cage.

No marks.
No metal.

"And this room?" Morales asked.

The man smiled.

"Storage. I emptied it yesterday. My wife complained about the smell."

Morales looked at him, uneasy.

"What smell?"

"Dampness. You know… Florida."

The woman checked the backyard.

There was no post.
No chain.
No bucket.

Only turned soil in one corner, covered with a sack of fertilizer.

"That?" she asked.

The man crouched, lifted the sack.

"Fertilizer. Look at this shitty soil."

The supervisor nodded, satisfied.

"No direct evidence."

Morales tightened his grip on the folder.

"But the pattern—"

"There is no visible animal," the woman said.

"Then we close it as 'no findings.'"

The supervisor took out a pen and signed.

The proper man walked everyone to the exit.

"Thank you for the work you do. We need to keep the neighborhood peaceful."

Morales got into the van without saying anything.

As they drove away, he looked in the rear-view mirror.

The chaotic yard was still there.

But the rectangle of soil looked darker than ever.

As if something were breathing underneath it.

CHAPTER 19 — The Proper Man

The neighborhood loves proper men.

Not because they are good.

Because they serve as curtains.

The following week a community meeting appeared in the park.

Folding chairs.
Cheap coffee.
A flag hanging from a table.

The proper man stood at the front.

He spoke clearly.
Smiled.
Used soft words.

"Security."
"Cameras."
"Watchful neighbors."
"Youth programs."

People applauded because applauding is easier than accusing.

Morales arrived late and stayed in the back.

He saw Ruiz taking notes.

“What is this?” Morales whispered.

Ruiz did not look at him.

“Damage control.”

The proper man raised his voice.

“We don’t want rumors. We want facts.”

The word *facts* dropped like a stone.

Morales felt disgust.

Because he knew what it meant:

that what is invisible does not exist.

“If anyone hears noises,” the proper man said, “call. But don’t invent stories.”

The women nodded.
The men tightened their mouths.

An old woman raised her hand.

“And the dogs?”

The proper man smiled, perfect.

“Almost nobody has dogs here. You know… order. Cleanliness.”

Small laughter.

Ruiz wrote: “successful meeting.”

The Magnolia case was officially closed three days later.

“Lack of evidence.”

An elegant sentence to say:

“It is more comfortable not to see.”

That same night, in the chaotic yard, someone dragged something heavy across the ground.

There were no screams.

They never lasted long.

CHAPTER 20 — Jesus Stops Being Useful

Jesus the Abuser knew something had changed when no one called.

Before, messages arrived fast.
A word.
A number.
A corner.

Now—silence.

Silence was worse than fear.
Fear still recognized him.
Silence *took his place*.

He looked at himself in the bathroom mirror.

The old wound in his side was closed on the outside.
Inside, it wasn't.

Sometimes his body still trembled.
No permission needed.

He washed his face.
He washed his hands.
He washed them too long.

As if water could give him his function back.

He went out.

The neighborhood looked at him… less.

It wasn't respect.
It was worn-out habit.

On the corner he saw the proper man.

Clean shirt.
Real watch.
A calibrated smile.

He was talking with two younger guys.
They laughed.

Jesus walked up.

"What's up?"

The proper man looked at him the way you look at an old chair.

"All good."

All good.
The perfect phrase.
The phrase that leaves you outside.

Jesus clenched his jaw.

"No one told me."

The proper man didn't raise his voice.

"Because there's no need."

Jesus felt the hollow open.

"What do you mean, no need?"

The proper man lifted a hand—calm.

"You're hot."
"You're nervous."
"And you're drawing attention."

Jesus swallowed.

"I'm the one who—"

The proper man cut him off. Soft. Precise.

"You're noise."

The word took the air out of him.

Right then a kid ran past on the sidewalk.
Tripped.

A man shouted after him:

"Ehhh!"

The sound.

The same sound from the dream.

Jesus went still—because for the first time he heard it from the outside.

The kid shut up.
Learned.

The proper man leaned closer.

"See?" he said.
"They don't need you to teach that anymore."

Jesus took one step back.

Not fear.

Vertigo.

That night he didn't play music.

He listened.

Behind a closed door, metal made a small sound.

The cage.

But it wasn't his cage anymore.

The whole house felt borrowed.

And Jesus understood the most offensive thing:

They weren't punishing him.

They were discarding him.

CHAPTER 21 — Social Metamorphosis

The ex-Ranger did not celebrate when the case was closed.

Because it had never been a case.

It had been a mechanism.

That morning he watered his plants with the same calm as always.

Water fell into dark soil with a small sound.
He crouched and touched a leaf.

The leaf didn't tremble.

That was enough.

Then he opened his notebook.

He read his own notes.

He wasn't looking for an ending.

He was looking for the replacement.

Because violence doesn't die.

It relocates.

The official visit had been clean.

Too clean.

That confirmed what he already knew:

Someone had guided the system toward the harmless.

He wrote one line:

"Magnolia has an administrator now."

He closed the notebook.

He looked down the street.

A new sign hung from a pole:

"NEIGHBORHOOD SAFETY PROGRAM."

Cameras.
Smiles.
Proper hands.

Everything looked more presentable.

That was the metamorphosis.

Crime hadn't disappeared.

It had learned how to dress.

That night the ex-Ranger passed near the chaotic yard.

He didn't stop.
He didn't stare.

He only listened.

A dry impact.
Like wood against concrete.

Then water.

Washing.

Always washing.

In a corner where the light never fully reached, the darkness seemed to adjust itself.

Not a figure.
Not a body.

An absence darker than the wall.

The Shadow didn't touch anything.

It only shifted posture—like someone taking a new seat.

The ex-Ranger understood, without emotion:

Jesus the Abuser had been an instrument.

Now the instrument was someone else.

Quieter.
More proper.
More dangerous.

And in that discovery he didn't feel defeat.

He felt assignment.

CHAPTER 22 – Epilogue: The Dog Who Doesn't Appear

After everything,
The ex-Ranger went back to his garden.

Not to escape.

To work.

There were things the system couldn't erase:

soil,
water,
patience.

He planted another seed.

He dug a small hole.
Set the seed inside.
Covered it with black earth.

He watered.

He watched the water enter dry ground.

He thought about the dog that never appeared in reports.

The dog who, to exist, had to be visible.

And then he thought the opposite:

The invisible lives, too.

The invisible leaves marks.

You just have to learn how to see them.

He opened the kitchen drawer.

The old leash was still there.

Worn leather.
Folded many times.

He didn't touch it.

He never did.

Not from pain.

From debt.

Under the turned soil, an old rusted ring was still tied to nothing.

He sat down.

He waited.

And when night came, the neighborhood settled into its usual normal:

dishes,
radios,
a brief laugh,
a weak argument.

Like a clean bandage over a dirty wound.

At 3:12, the Ranger opened his eyes.

Not because he heard a whimper.

Because he heard something worse—

trained silence.

He listened.

And inside that silence, in a language he did understand, a tiny sound arrived.

Not a bark.
Not a cry.

A light metal tap—almost shy—against tile.

The ex-Ranger sat up.

Feet on cold floor.

He took his notebook and wrote:

“3:12 / it’s back.”

He closed the notebook.

He pulled on his pants without turning on the light.

He took his keys.

Not his phone.

And he went out.

Because his war was never an explosion.

It was persistence.

www.ingramcontent.com/pod-product-compliance
Lightning Source LLC
LaVergne TN
LVHW090528110826
845146LV00003B/1019

* 9 7 9 8 9 9 4 0 7 3 2 5 4 *